MW00872517

I Am Love
In Memory of
Andrew O'Hearn Toon

By Andrew O'Hearn Toon

Edited by Tabatha Jenkins

ISBN: **1545504458**
ISBN-13: **978-1545504451**

"As grim as it sounds, we are winning and we shall be victorious. Why? Because God has come out to join our struggle. The God within each of us is ready for battle.....and the God within us is what we must count on until a cure is found."

-Andrew O'Hearn Toon

February 5th, 1965 – December 22nd, 1992

CONTENTS

Introduction
by Nancy Stephens Toon

As parents of three sons my husband and I cherished each one. Our beloved middle son, Andrew, died in 1992 of AIDS. We watched him fight a courageous battle with this awful disease. He was able to keep his humor in some very trying situations. He was "laughing all the way" and tried to keep us upbeat.

Andy was a happy baby, child, and adult even though he faced people who were often judgmental and hateful. He had a wonderful way of meeting criticism with humor. Fortunately there were many more people who treated him with love and kindness. He could at times react with a kind of sarcasm that was not always understood. He had a brilliant mind and loved to write.

His father died seven years after Andy's death. We had often discussed where his talents might have taken him. He was a leader/organizer and loved politics and parties. At the end of his life he was very involved in AIDS Education. He not only wrote on the subject, but visited schools and churches to talk to young people. Some of the young people and many of Andy's friends encouraged me to publish some of his literary works. After twenty-five years, I have decided to gather and publish some of his work. There are so many boxes of notes, letter, photos, poetry, and news articles that he had collected that it has been difficult to make selections. Hopefully the publication can be shared with family and friends who stood by us. He probably would rather have done it his way, but "Mama tried". Our Methodist Church supported and encouraged our family in so many ways. Members of the medical field never wavered in seeking ways to treat Andy and he became a symbol for some to aggressively seek better treatments and a cure for him.

I am grateful for the guidance of the University of Arkansas at Monticello's Creative Writing Department. A very gifted senior writing student, Tabatha Jenkins, took this on as a senior project. It was good to meet with Tabatha as she patiently made suggestions.

Editor's Note

This collection includes the life's work of Andrew O'Hearn Toon. Throughout his life, Andrew was an avid writer of poetry and short stories. He was also a photographer and a fierce activist. His writing ranges in theme from serious to sarcastic and witty. This represents the different voices that Andrew demonstrated in his writing. This is the first time that any of his writing will be published. This book also includes a short biography, his personal letters and correspondences, and remarks from his family and friends.

This project was presented to me through one of my professors at the University during my senior year. During the course of my last semester I met with Mrs. Toon several times in order to organize this collection and decide the route we wanted to pursue to publish it.

I am very grateful for Mrs. Toon's patience, hard work, and for trusting me with her son's work. I have tried my best to stay true to Andrew's work and put together a publication that would represent him justly.

I would also like to acknowledge the University of Arkansas at Monticello's Creative Writing Department for giving me this opportunity to learn a great deal about the editing world. I would like to thank Dr. Craig Olsen for his help and Alannah Hensley for her much appreciated advice and guidance.

POETRY

I AM WHO I AM

I don't fall in love…

I become love. And in doing so,

becoming love,

it is a task I tend

to perfect.

A perfect love

that surrounds what was

once my shell,

and melts it with

a becoming warmth.

Upon realization,

(upon the end)

I ignore such poets

who do not go gently

into that good night.

For upon realization,

upon becoming love,

I know purpose and destiny:

not rebellion.

(although the love that I am

is rebellion within itself)

There is no love I feel…

I don't fall in love.

I am who I am

in an ethereal sense of being,

in an ethereal sense,

I am love.

UPCOMING FUNERAL

My family wants

me to write

a poem

for my dying great-

grandmother.

(for her funeral)

A beautiful poem

to salt

the wounds.

GENESIS

Don't be so shallow

as to think that

Death ends it all.

Death, as they say,

my boy,

is only the beginning,

And,

In the beginning…

(You know the rest from there)

BATTLE HYMN OF THE REPUBLIC

(EVERY 12ᵗʰ LETTER ONLY)

eyoit   hrfr

ou   f   s

ie   eor T

       e

drgs

snili

 i   r

reltm

demsiGgueostu;

aeki

i

(a sixth stanza was written by the author but is seldom

quoted)

INDEPENDENCE (98 YEARS)

The funeral was over,

and I sat,

alone,

on the back porch.

My own problems

engulfing my

existence like

a cult movement.

98 years

is a long time.

I think she thought so too.

But all seems

like wind,

and the tractor

surpasses my thoughts

by producing

the smell of

wet morning hay.

And she enjoyed that smell,

like a country declaration

of independence.

ESTELLE'S IRONY

Estelle

is old.

She repeats her

stories of pioneer life

over and over

but we all nod

and politely listen.

She'll be dead soon.

And we'll long for

her repetition.

STAY TUNED

you Loved me

like A tv

evangelist,

but I goT smart and

chAnged

chanNels.

CLEAR POEM

(OPAQUE PUNCTUATION)

,

.

;

,   .

.

TRIBUTE TO WARHOL

3 subject

notebook

10 ½ In. X 8 In. 120 Sheets

3 sections/ 40 sheets Each

Wide Marginal Ruled

BUS TRIP

Traveling by bus

I sit alone.

A sign by the window

reads;

Lift this bar,

Push window open.

I realize the window

and I

are one

while the girl in

the next seat reads Vogue.

The next day,

I sit

somewhere else.

COMPOSER

They wouldn't

have called

Vivaldi a genius

if there had been

5 seasons

and he had forgotten one.

He would have been

labeled

a fool.

GODOT'S ARRIVAL

I knew you were coming so

I baked a cake. Maybe.

(at this point the cake falls,

and is thrown in Godot's face.

Godot shoots self.

Before dying, looks at watch.

On seeing he is late, he laughs.

Other characters move. Curtain.)

MATILDA'S PASSION

She saw it

22 times and

cried every time.

Her mother paid her way.

"I love the special effects"

Her mother bought the popcorn.

"Let's sit closer to the front, dear"

Her mother got new glasses.

"He's so cute. I can't believe he dies"

Her mother sighed and ate all the popcorn.

"Tomorrow is the last show, dear"

Her mother was thankful.

"Maybe they'll re-release it"

Her mother cried.

REFLECTION ON ELEMENTARY SCHOOL

I will not talk in class.

I will not talk in class.

I will not talk in class.

I will not talk in class.

I will not talk in class.

I will not talk in class.

I will not talk in class.

I will not talk in class.

I will not talk in class.

I will not talk in class.

x 10.

PARIS PICNIC

On our way to Paris

we stopped in Chartres

and bought food

for a picnic.

The trail that led

through the wood

was ivy-covered,

and muddy,

outside Paris.

POETRY CLASS

My professor told me

what the poem meant.

I went home and

dipped

the poem in blue paint.

covered

it with glue.

stuck it to the wall.

threw

wet spiders and willow leaves at it.

burned

it with a blow torch.

used

the ashes in a salad.

My view of the poem

was quite different from his.

I got more out of it.

PARTY CONVERSATIONS

Well, we are all here.

Well, here we all are.

Are we all, well here.

We are all well, here.

All we, are well here.

We all here well, are.

Here, well we all are.

All here, well we are.

We all, well are here.

Well, we are all here.

I STEP INTO THE WOODS

The soap-opera love-life

of a mule-deer continues

as the skunk contemplates suicide

because his best ally,

the garter-snake,

was killed by a hedge-hog.

    I step into the woods,

    and the melodrama ceases.

    Animals

    will be

    animals.

Who knows what goes on

when we aren't around?

    I'll bet the ants could tell you.

LETTER FROM A YOUNGER COUSIN

Dear Andy how are

you dooing Andy

how are thanes goin

going Andy how are

thanges going Andy

I love you Andy I

want you to write me

a letter Andy I

want you to see you

Andy I love you

Andy how are

you dooing Andy

how are thanes

going Andy love you.

CITY PARANOIA

He falls

down the street

busy with midnight

traffic

and hustlers

(body and soul)

with a

Michael Jackson

sock on one foot

and none on the other.

He suddenly stops

and realizes

he is dead.

Brushing this off

as a joke,

he continues.

But notices that

no one seems to

look at him.

Being dead is easy

in the ghetto.

POINT (OVERHEARD AS CAMUS SPOKE TO MILTON, SORT OF)

do you realize you

are dying

every day and you

enjoy death's slow

process, its razor

teeth slowing slicing?

It gives you time

to suffer a fate

more horrible than

Death.

You live to die.

You die to live.

and it should have

been called Paradise

Hidden.

A FLIRT ON PARADE

As simple as it can be

why ignore it?

Foolish black cat.

You can't hide it even if

yourunyourwordstogether.

Silly black cat.

Prrrrrrrrrrrrrrr

is your answer to

your problems.

People like you are, well,

you know,

funny little black cat.

eyes a-glowing with wantoness.

Black, black cat.

Cross a path too soon, my dear,

and You will wind up as

another part of the pavement,

Stupid Blac Kat.

NEW GENERATION

They look back

on Beaver.

we look back

on Sonny and Cher.

"And that has made all the difference."

ON MY ATLAS

How do they decide

which state is

      which

color?

This has bothered me for years.*

*I have not tried to write the

publishers.

EXCERPTS FROM ORIENTATION SPEECH

(UNIVERSITY OF ARKANSAS AT FAYETTEVILLE)

a general course

let me read let me ask

i have the same questions

home mortgages

more practical

consistent grading scale

the question is…

what's the difference?

those students who want

many who are interested

creative imagination needed

pursue that yes you could

the last year or so

would be happy to tell you

programs not unlike that

not necessarily a variety of fields

do we have a list

in the beginning

it may be necessary

you should be careful

in these activities

i would have no objections

should be possible

other questions?

i was curious whats the limit

in conjunction with

let me thank you

once again

IN AUTUMN SLAUGHTER

When I asked you,

your eyes said

that you were

Deer

paused on hoof

in autumn slaughter

listening (once again)

for the quickness

of the dogs.

COUPONS

the sun-brown colour

of the keyboard

of the register

matches the sneer

within her eyes

and compliments

her polyester.

ZEALOT

At the airport

I was given a

book by a man

named Chandi Das.

He signed it.

It has some

wonderful colour pictures

of Indian art.

CHRIST

(APPLAUSE)

A TABLESPOON TO DROWN

I sense evil in the rain today.

Around here, and elsewhere,

there are those convinced of the smell of rain,

convinced of some sort of dampness, an odor,

of trees and yellow insects in a storm

which leads to translation

like religious tongues in pentecostal fevers.

I found that conviction in the rain today.

I feared for my life on the route to town.

Have you ever seen so much rain

on the lips of the earth

in July, my neighbor? A child

only needs a tablespoon to drown.

In sordid lumps the mill continues,

ignorant of evil showers.

Today the strike ended. It never really happened.

And what do you call hay

before you cut it down?

Around here, and elsewhere,

violet sheets cover houses as I lay here,

sniffing out evil

and hoping all against dampened snakes

and preying for the dogs:

silence is my sound.

JOE

He went through high school

(and life for that matter)

with a mirror over his face.

It reflects patrons,

mostly.

CHEERLEADER

she saves

her corsages

from dates.

SO TODAY IS TUESDAY

Nothing is so special

in the world as tuesday.

Every week I hide behind

17, 18, 19, dates, 20, 21,

holding everything in the hope

of another tuesday.

I may be odd, but

I've got my Tuesdays.

What do you have to call your own?

CHAIRS FOR DAYS

Sorry. It's an

inside joke.

Just me and my

friends know.

Maybe I'll tell

you later.

JOURNAL

It was what she wrote in.

It was where she felt.

Her Capote still-life

hardens brick-breath

to my bonded heart.

Barbara never said love so eloquently.

Barbara never called me on that one.

Barbara kept it to herself.

Typing my eyes in place,

spacing my mouth out,

kissing me within the margins

with 11:00 stanza lips

and that Jerry Lewis

rip-off brassiere.

Treating barbeque like a lover,

eating divinity.

Barbara made quotations

in the air

too soon

for clever translations.

She never said love so eloquently

as her silence.

ANNIVERSARY

He has tilted ideas

of broken headlamps

on antique cars

when he thinks of

the way his

grandmother spent time.

Her deep, black bodice

whips his leg

in thoughts of

soldiers on Normandy Beach.

His grandmother's spent task

of several children proved her downfall

and caused…

Caused the beach

to swell,

with redundant sequence.

LESLIE

She's wonderful

And attractive.

1980-1984

4 yrs ago she ws

Homecoming Queen

last wk she ws charged

w/shoplftng in a grocry

stre.

And it goes nd gs.

CHIP

He met

a famous

person at

a party.

I'm jealous.

UNTITLED

unpoem

TOSSED BLESSINGS

A calm, cool juice supporting sailboats

of thoughts, of Paul Revere, of beer cans (red and tan)

sustains his evangelical,

his somewhat spiritual purpose.

    Am I too late for the polling?

    Have the saints gone marching in?

    Or are we still waiting for the bean dip?

Impertinent: quite imperfect.

He sails by the masses, riding the crest of grey foam,

riding the crest of compulsive (yet charming) guilt.

    Kowabunga! Kowajesus! Khristabunga!

And the solemn mother-of-three with her good will:

And the naked mother-of-three in tears over spilled milk

floats by in a dog paddle stride

full of nothing but sincerity

which (as we all know)

sinks to the bottom first

in the calm, cool juice of world champions.

    She gets a round on the house

    and the next round

    goes

    on your tab.

ROGER

has always

acted like that.

Even in high school,

his friends just

laughed it

off.

HISTORY IN PERSPECTIVE

Roosevelt was a cripple.

SOUR FRIENDSHIP

is to me what

jim jones did for

punch.

AND NOT ONLY THAT

but I am still

in shock that

Buffy Overdosed

PASSIONATE THOUGHTS

Bathing in

love lines

and subtle

hints

of coming

allusions

DEPICTER

marilyn withstood time

with whirling warhol colors wild

and andy gave her

the yellow hair life

and cherry lip look

of damsel legend distressed.

Subway wind romance

of fake laughter itches.

Something Gave.

LOTS O' MAKE-UP

Dawn works in

a clothing store. She won't sell

men's clothes to

women

or visa versa.

She thinks that's sick.

ON ENTERING ADULTHOOD

Mom seems shorter.

HUMANITY

…it all

comes down to

hairstyles…

FREUDIAN INTERFERENCE

Then there are those

childhood moments.

You are so

unsure,

praying

that the horrid

images

were dreams

and not reality.

CARD GAMES

You will have your chance.

Chance:

when we all go

to a funeral.

You never really

<u>knew</u> them.

You just make

large circles

with your emotions,

playing cards

on a

Saturday night funeral game.

You will have your chance.

I had mine.

STATE SLOGAN

AR is a

    natural

       <u>what?</u>

RERUN

Looking back,

I can see

it was

Gilligan's fault.

Nobody with

any brains would

enjoy being

pelted by

an overweight slob.

Some people deserve it.

BREAKFAST

With eyes

like a dead toaster,

you watch

in Pop-tart

primness.

DEBUTANTE OF A FALLEN SOCIETY

They try not

to notice

Cornelia's

double chin.

FROM CITY TO THE SAME

His face

represented that

thin   line

between supply and demand.

Traffic rushes across

his chin

at 8:35 AM

seconds before the rush

of non-moving cars.

When he yawns,

my condo brushes

his nostrils

in a perilous conquest

of unleaded interstate.

PHOTO ALBUM

images grow

continuously

from my blue as

blossoming new plants in

a universal herbal garden.

Each new image

fragrantly wafts the

wind of chance.

My Kodak memory collects

yellow ones

and makes the

moment lasts

in blue.

WHY I LOVE YOU

the phone is

answered

on the

sixth sadistic ring.

LATE NIGHT SNACK

I sit under formica,

atring at your contacts.

Renaissance springs life into your laugh.

You drive me insane

with the eating of a burger:

a burger reconciled.

DORMITORY LIFE

He was

brushing his teeth

at 3:31 AM

when I asked

what the hell

are you doing?

Brushing my teeth

says he.

Oh says I.

HOLLYWOOD REALITY

If it's only a

paper moon,

then how come

Ryan beats

his kids?

GRANDMOTHER THOUGHTS

It attacks with

memories in

skins and

candy bars and

rubber bands,

forming a macrame' tear

in Look magazine.

MADNESANITYCHOTIC

Molly can't sleep

that fly on the wall.

He screams

at the breadth

of his lungs.

She can't stand

bad opera

by

small insects.

I WANT TO GO BACK TO HALY

(OR A NOTE FOUND IN A LIBRARY BOOK)

Just enjoying a nice evening at home (Karen's out

on a blind date), listening to Pino Danielle in your

bathrobe. Wishing my ChiChi would write. Just read

an article in an old Playgirl Miss Kayren gave me

about unhip men. I want one. I am so tired of

swingers who dress and talk prep and OU football games.

I had such a good time in LR – it was also

good to see you guys in Conway.

I'm sending along this letter I got from Chris – I

enjoyed it.

I don't have much on my mind –

ramona

GIDDY

She bounced

from wall to wall

like a small pinhead spider

in a helium balloon.

TIM

A guy who firmly believes

he should have been born in Nam.

He knows

the people,

battles,

places.

He believes firmly.

SOCIO-WEIGHTLIFTING

The intertwining feeling

of halocaustic smiles

envelope your sunken face.

I was watching a game show

and you were cleaning an ashtray (ironic)

when it happened.

A woman from Sacramento

who enjoys crocheting

won a cancer from long-time exposure.

A man from Buffalo (vacationing at the time)

won baldness.

We,

on the other hand, were closer.

I literally filled my shoes,

and you became ashes

for your freshly-cleaned tray.

(digging your own grave, so to speak)

Timing was so perfect.

It makes you laugh at its

Mr. America image.

CHUCK

Now he is

trying to grow

his hair

longer.

Speeding 4:11 AM

Caesar would have

had that cop

beheaded

for giving <u>him</u>

a ticket.

LIMERICK

There once was a man dada da,

Da da dada da dada da.

Da da dada da,

Da da dada da,

Da da dada da dada God.

JUSTIFICATION

In due process,

your life is made

like a turbine-driven ego

running down the freeway

of a bigot's mind.

Subsequent events wheel

from rest area to restaurant

turning the courtroom

into your apartment.

FILM

My little brother sat nude

in a cardboard box

posed with our beagle,

Snoopy,

as mother took a picture.

SOMETIMES YOU WIN

On the instant

highway,

he saw a car

in the approach.

Her face was not

well-formed,

but he knew

he hated her,

so he swerved

into the other lane.

Sometimes you lose.

ALL ABOUT EARTHQUAKES

In conversation

(the other day)

someone said,

Consider California.

I didn't want to

Consider California.

So I didn't.

I missed the point

of the conversation,

but I feel

much better

about myself,

and I think

I am still stable.

I'm worried that

someday

I <u>will</u>

Consider California,

then I'll be forced

to change my being.

SURVIVAL

trailing after

delusions in

a grid-iron web

of larger delusions,

the essentials

seems so sudden

in coming

to your rescue

only to

charge interest

later

LOSS OF WORDS

with only

my left

shoe

to stare at.

AT A PARTY

You mentioned India.

Why?

A WORD

Hello

IT'S A SMALL WORLD

Yesterday,

I used the word

DELVE

three times in an hour.

The event left me quite shaken.

Such words are too tender

to use so often.

I had wounded

a vocabulary Florence Nightingale.

CONCEIT

my being

plunges

my interiors

into rhapsody

ANDREW

Causes

incomplete

to think

me to

senten

DEATH BY QUARTZ

I reach across the face from my 2,

(you are standing on 7)

but the second hand swipes

my grasp.

You are on the far side

Of the expanse

Of my Timex:

dancing like a crystalline Mickey,

living in hour-hand motion.

I could go on,

but it's dinnertime.

The expansion of my Timex

doth decree.

COOKIE

Like a

McDonaldland cookie,

you grow stale

in my

oscillating fan breeze,

for humidity

makes Ronald's make-up run.

DREW (AUTOBIOGRAPHY)

It was half price

so I bought

2

DELUSIONS

hidden away and

deep in my mind's mind.

how far does it go?

to the bone?

or am I merely waiting

out my time in a

phantom cell

made of several items that

I hate...

don't forget that I am delude-

d,

and this is all a

draem(oops)dream

PSYCHIC PLEA

No one takes me seriously

when I say,

I think I'm dying or something.

They just say,

cheerup!

Huh, cheer up, sure.

THE BEST QUESTION EVER
PUT FORTH TO ME

Sure, Drew is fine,

but how is Drew?

-Dave Fleming

VANDALISM

When George Segal

made it,

who ever dreamed

of a sledge hammer?

Art is

everchanging

what it is,

and a new look

is a new

look.

BEGINNING OF SUMMER

2 people

and a blue fan

seems so natural

without

air conditioning.

Neither person

likes the colour

of the fan.

But it

must be

withstood.

SIMILE

Like a left-handed desk,

you wipe the blood

from your nose

onto your multi-coloured sleeve.

Your enemy runs away

like a nun on drugs,

as you kill him with

your motorized eyes.

DALLY THOUGHTS

Dark horse colour of

the civil war haircut

blends smoothly with

the jellybean taste

of his pseudo-fingers.

In smooth looks of

broken carpet/ he catches

the falling stars

with his mouth, and he

dallies on the door-step.

DAY OF DEMOTION

you are

a golden

smoking jacket

that Sammie Davis

threw away.

You'll never fit

in style again.

Like Elvis' collars.

TOURIST

Trying so hard

in a

I (heart) NY

sweatshirt.

I want to help,

but

she is so

unique:

I like to watch

her struggle

with hair colours.

MEDITATION ON CLONING

Ditto.

CRUXIFICTION

Back shot back

to the gods of time

(if such exists)

time plays on water (and sand)

gut feelings of

substantiated monetary

units. Fall turns

to fall. Back

shot back.

Robber guy robber.

Guy robber guy.

10$ off on

shackle blood mother.

VIGIL

Small doorway

covered in black.

Flower stench stings in air.

They talk behind

her dead back.

(good talk, though)

Nice make-up.

They moved the television

into Helen's room

to get the casket

in the den.

Marie sleeps on

as Aunt Hazel

arranges her arms.

Dessert was served

in the kitchen.

REMARKABLE SPARK

She has a

remarkable spark

of human vanity.

Two weeks later,

after brain surgery

(the same killed her sister)

she would not allow

visitors.

No hair or wig yet.

Her vanity is

hope for hair.

VET

The new generation

missed the point.

He named his first-born son

Napalm

in protest.

All the kids now just say,

God, what a stupid name.

WHAT'S IN A NAME

My closest friend

(at this writing)

is named John Wayne.

He has a sister

named Loretta Lynn.

I can't think of a *thing*

to write about the situation.

So I won't.

His mother tongue-tied me

before I go to

attack with cynicism.

I'll just let the

name hold its own.

-October 1st, 1984

NEW LEASE

They say society's child

has no claim to liability.

The truth:

society is completely to blame.

ex:

Do you know how hard it is

to be born

18 years after your birth

just because

you had to wear clothes

just so

instead of

your way?

STEREO

A Sondheim wind

blows, wafts, bounds,

across a sensual field

of inherit intellect greenery.

In one motion,

in one accord,

tune straining against tune

in molasses speed.

A quick blur.

Volume up.

Sondheim to mayhem

in one accord,

as art should be.

IN THE END, THE FINAL COUNT

Getting a postcard from

Helen, Bob, and the kids,

doesn't make me a god,

but it does count for something.

EVOLUTION

Sometimes I watch my goldfish,

Sedgewick and Dallesandro Smith,

gulp air from the water's surface.

They, are trying to evolve,

I am thinking.

I can tell that

they

are bothered by the fact

they

must first become amphibious.

They

are working hard on evolving.

THE DIFFERENT DAY

I took a nap

at 1:30

in the afternoon

(a new concept to me)

I woke up

confused,

stiff,

and got in

my car

and drove to

the grocery store.

I then realized

I had no business

there.

Moral:

don't sleep in

the afternoon.

Confusion creeps in

like the receipt

from your grocery bill.

BANG! FALL DOWN

You can't have peace

as long as

children play army.

And they always have.

And they always will.

Nothing bores a child faster

than the game

of peace.

VISITING HOME (FARM AFTER CHILDHOOD)

Standing near

my father,

he talks about

my life (throwing it

away, etc.)

we stand near

the sewer.

A dead cow is

between us.

He is happy here.

The vet will come soon

to perform an autopsy.

id

The difference between

a smile and a scowl

is so minute,

it makes one wonder

if there is any

difference

at all.

DIVINE PNEMONIA

I find it odd

that a god so

human

never sneezed.

(at least he

never let it

be known.)

TRIBUTE TO MY PARENTS

You seems so

factually unreal.

Like a 1968

World Book

Encyclopedia.

So much you say

is true about

Yugoslavia

and

Herbert Hoover.

But the models

with the cat-eye glasses

and guys with

engulfing sideburns

make you

surrealistic

in a dictionary

sort-of-way.

COUNTRY LIFE PERSISTENCE

It is times like these

you forget

if those damned

hostages will make it,

and glory in

a farmland sunrise

over evergreens

and barn top roofs.

Times like these,

you lose your

conscience to

country life persistence.

TIME IS THAT MOMENT

Time is that

moment you

forgot to

set the alarm.

The ethereal sunrise

rolled over

your head

without warning.

A moment

is granted

retribution

for so many

lost years

and

hidden metaphors.

THINGS TO DIE WITH

Keep a secret on a friend,

Tell it at journey's end.

Tell it when the trip's not through,

Makes an enemy of you.

I hate to write that type of poetry, but it seemed the only

appropriate way to convey the message.

1.

OH, SAY

Can you see?

I can't tell.

You never look

this way.

2.

BY THE DAWN'S EARLY LIGHT

Problems confer convention-like.

They do not refrain from violence.

They take no coffee breaks.

They simply count grains

on a beach of gray matter

in morning tide.

3.

WE HAILED

I pseudo-worshipped

philosophy

of a different colour.

So proudly, we hailed cinema gods

in red velvet chairs.

4.

IN THE TWILIGHT'S LAST GLEAMING

I was reading

Jack said

Marta was

cooking chicken.

A shot was fired.

I read.

Jack said.

The chicken never flinched.

Marta went to the hospital

as a joke.

The gun was

full of blanks.

A vicious feather-of-revenge

had aimed.

10.

YET WAVING, STILL THERE

After it all,

after the plastic money

after the tax hikes,

the star spangled banner

remains

in the second rack

of a dry cleaners.

Our flag (STAND UP!)

is being cleaned

while

redemption

stalks the streets.

12.

HOME OF THE BRAVE

A vision was birthed

Yesterday,

stillborn.

It is not

in the infirmary.

It has been disposed of

before naming.

SHORT STORIES

Linen In Her Eyes

Sometimes I look at myself and I think I have the whole world in terms of pro- or anti-polyester images, and someone always comes along and wrecks my melancholy realism.

The realism is that Cassandra (a three-year-old cousin) has an endearing smile and it lights up the mornings like Brando did cigarettes in movies.

The realism is that it is so sickeningly wonderful to see a child that is happy with life.

It makes you wish you didn't know the truth about the horrors of polyester. Your sermon, your whole damned presentation, on its evils leave Cassandra's eyes unscathed.

The linen in her eyes accounts for me.

-Andrew O'Hearn Toon

What Happened To Baby Jane

The classroom was "normal size". Since it was the first grade and therefore the first classroom, I took it for granted that this was a normal size classroom. I have forever based classes on that one. One word in that room has determined my educational future.

Apparently, I was a very good student. They would have called my gifted back then, but that would have been positive reinforcement and there was a law against such. I think.

Anyway, myself, a boy named Billy, and a girl named Shannon were eventually separated from the rest of the class like so many marshmallows in cocoa. We were different from the others. We read faster.

Close to the end of the year, Mrs. Finley had us reading at a sixth grade level. But I jumped the metaphorical gun. It was in my early reading where I encountered that word, that one word that I have based my existence.

By now, you are probably on the edge of your metaphorical seat wondering what the word could be. Relax. Smoke a cigarette, have a screwdriver, and prepare thyself for the word   enough.

The story that included the word (the word being "enough" for those of you not paying attention) was about a lark named Mark who barked in the dark. From there, I think you can tell that we were working on the –ar sound. If you didn't realize that fact, then I will also tell you that Mark had a shark friend by the name of Clark who gave off sparks.

In the story, the word appeared. I don't know why or where. All I can tell you is that it appeared like the maid in *Whatever Happened To Baby Jane?* except Bette's hammer was missing (I being Bette). I became Joan, the word lying at the foot of my bed, so close to comprehension, but my mouth is taped.

I didn't understand a single thing about the word except how to use it in context when speaking to humans. I didn't understand why it was spelled so. Its spelling had nothing to do with its sound. It had nothing to do with the sage of Mark and Clark. The definition itself was wrong. There can never be enough by definition.

That was the beginning of my school career. I know that if I would have comprehended that one word, my education would be over. Some nights I stay up wondering what would have happened if

I would have comprehended. For years now I have avoided the word completely in hopes of continuing my ignorance. It is frightening to know that your very existence is hinged on one word. But there is also a morbid security in knowing that to exist in peace with Mrs. Crawford, one only has to avoid enough.

-Andrew O'Hearn Toon

LETTERS & CORRESPONDENCES

During his life, Andrew wrote several letters, most of these to his family and friends. However, he also wrote letters to newspapers, TV stations, even the House of Representatives. He even wrote a letter to the President of the Philippines. Most of these he received replies to.

Andrew was an activist, specifically for the AIDS community. He spent the majority of his later life trying to raise awareness for this disease that he suffered from and that ultimately claimed his life.

He was an outspoken, fearless, young man who had an incredible way with words. He was also incredibly family-oriented and always had his family members on his mind.

ACTIVIST AND EDITORIAL LETTERS

TOMMY F. ROBINSON
2D DISTRICT, ARKANSAS

COMMITTEES:
EDUCATION AND LABOR
POST OFFICE AND CIVIL SERVICE
SELECT COMMITTEE ON CHILDREN,
YOUTH, AND FAMILIES

TAX POLICY & JOB OPPORTUNITIES
TASK FORCE
CHAIRMAN

WASHINGTON OFFICE:
1541 LONGWORTH HOB
WASHINGTON, DC 20515-0402
(202) 225-2506

Congress of the United States
House of Representatives
Washington, DC 20515-0402

February 28, 1990

Mr. Drew Toon
103 South Woodrow
Little Rock, AR 72205

Dear Mr. Toon:

Thank you for contacting me to express your opposition to the basing of the Peacekeeper Rail Garrison at Little Rock Air Force Base. I appreciate your taking the time to let me know how you feel.

As you probably know, the Air Force has officially chosen Little Rock Air Force Base as a Rail Garrison sight.

I support the basing of the Peacekeeper at LRAFB. It will compensate for the loss of the 308th Titan Missile Wing which has been deactivated. The economic benefits to central Arkansas will be substantial. I also believe it is necessary to the defense of our nation to deploy a survivable, mobile missile. Although the Soviets have recently allowed radical change in the world, stability has not come to these regions of change. Therefore, a continued need for strategic defense remains. I am sorry we disagree on this issue, but please continue to let me know your thoughts and comments.

Sincerely,

Tommy F. Robinson

Tommy F. Robinson
Member of Congress

> Andrew wrote a letter to the House of Representatives opposing the basing of the Peacekeeper Rail Garrison at the Little Rock Air Force Base. This is the response that he received from Tommy F. Robinson, a member of Congress.

1527 FEDERAL BUILDING
700 WEST CAPITOL AVE.
LITTLE ROCK, AR 72201-3270
(501) 378-5941

411 NORTH SPRUCE
SEARCY, AR 72143-4222
(501) 268-4287

P.O. Box 431
LONOKE COUNTY COURTHOUSE
LONOKE, AR 72086-0431
(501) 676-6403

FAULKNER COUNTY COURTHOUSE
COUNTY JUDGE'S OFFICE
LOCUST ST.
CONWAY, AR 72032
(501) 327-6589

Office of the President
of the Philippines
Malacañang

May 31, 1990

MR. DREW TOON
103 S. Woodrow
Little Rock, Arizona 72205
U. S. A.

Dear Mr. Toon,

    Our research staff reports that according to the "Condensed Dictionary of Paper Terms and Terminology" published by the Association of Paper Traders of the Philippines, Manila envelope is defined as: "Fourdrinier M. F. Paper made in Manila color of chemical wood pulps with some percentage of mechanical wood pulps. Weight ranges from 60 to 150 GSM. It is used for conversion to envelopes mainly for commercial purposes." *

    On the other hand, Manila is defined as: "Term used to indicate color and finish compared to paper manufactured from Manila hemp stack."

    You are right - the Archbishop of Manila is Cardinal Sin. The Cardinal's complete name is Jaime Cardinal L. Sin.

Sincerely yours,

MARIA ASUNCION FERNANDO
Acting Head
Correspondence Office

* Fourdrinier M. F. is a machine named after its sponsor, normally used in the manufacture of all grades of paper and board.

This a response to a letter Andrew sent from Maria Asuncion Fernando, the Acting Head for the Correspondence Office for the President of the Philippines.

A new generation is upon us: a generation of young adults who vaguely know that "Woodstock" was something besides the name of Snoopy's sidekick; that a young politician named Kennedy had a very hidden private life; that Russia used to be more than a nuclear monger at one time. They don't have any rememberances of an alive Marilyn.

In the late forties, a young girl with semi-perfect teeth and frizzy hair began appearing in movies. From the beginning her talent for dramatic roles was hidden by her natural beauty. She was typecast by own face and body.

Ms. Monroe lived in a world of candid dreams that she often spoke of. She came to fame bearing a list of foster homes, and she told stories of abandment and abuse that would make Manson shiver. She was mentally, physically, and sexually abused in such a way that she would never be able to share her love, talent, and wealth with her offspring. The empty gap left by numerous operations and miscarraiges left Marilyn with a feeling of distrust of men, which was revealed in three abolished marraiges. Although she was flawed on the inside, Norma Jeane DiMaggio, as she was named on some official papers, could make her real life so invisible to the public that all they saw was a goddess. The Goddess of Love, of Temptation, of Humor, and of Sensuality.

Senuality had been around a long time before Marilyn was born, but no other actress in Hollywood's history could define it like she could. Marilyn has become an Easter Lily: beautiful, soft, but the reminder of a tragic event. Since August 2, 1962, there has arisen a new generation. This year, the children born in the same year as the Goddess' termination,(by her own hand), will turn 21.

Being part of the new generation, we fin d it hard to imagine the Marilyn that could have been. A Marilyn over 60 is not easy to picture. Death is the frame that has enhanced her beauty forever.

-2-

Many actresses will stain many rolls of film with images of their faces, but none will ever imitate the perfect imitator. None will reach that "Marilyn Point" of flawed perfection.

Andy Toon
Rt. 2 Box 335
Crossett, AR
71635

An Editorial written by Andrew regarding Marilyn Monroe. He spent three years researching Ms. Monroe's life.

FAMILY CORRESPONDENCES

Dec. 24, 1989

The Stephens family has made it through the 1980's. We began our lives here in Ashley County back in 1848, and we are now going into our 15th decade here.

The 1980's saw the passing of Big Mama, Mattie, Marie, Edgar, and Vera. There were several marriages, including Shannon and Mark, John and Sherri, Stella and James, and Norma and Marion. Born to us in this decade were David Maxwell, Anna Yauger, Ann Stephens, and Amy Yauger. We saw plenty of high school and college graduations, too numerous to list.

We began the 1980's with the release of the American hostages in Iran, we lived through the Reagan Years, and we are now ready for the 1990's: the last decade of this century. We are certainly off to a good start. With the demise of the Berlin Wall, the fall of the Eastern Bloc to democracy, and the hope of justice in Panama, we are ready for the new decade that could prove to be our greatest yet.

Everyone seems to be trying to predict the future of the world, but hey, that's easy to do. Anybody can predict:

-Elizabeth Taylor will marry Malcolm Forbes, Donald Trump, and Elvis.

-Governor Tommy Robinson will switch religions in order to get more votes.

Well, we want to know more important things than that, things that deal with our family, so we have enlisted the services of the Reverend Swami Origami Bahami Mommy. We will have the Swami compile a list of predictions for the future to be read aloud at the family gathering in 1999.

Andrew Toon

The Toon Family

September 27, 1991

Dear Kith and Kin,

I don't know quite where to begin this letter, but let me say that I am so proud of my family I don't know what to do. Your response to my illness just goes to show that we are a proud and loving unit of strong people. I could not have asked for a better family. I want you all to know how important it is to my health that I know I have your support. I know so many people who have horror stories to tell about their families. So many people have been turned away and left alone, and I have been blessed with thoughtful, caring relatives. Thanks so much for responding in a responsible and loving way to my disease.

I hate to bring it up, but there were some out there who made no response at all. I do not know whether or not this was because they did not know what to say or they resented me for my disease and sexual orientation. I know that the fear they feel comes from ignorance of the facts, and for what they don't know, I'll forgive them. But I want to point out that there are those who obviously are scared of me and willing to discriminate. I encourage those of you who understand to discuss this problem with those who are unsure. This family must move forward. Anyway, when Christmas rolls around, or the family reunion, you can bet I'll be asking some questions. I want to know why some can accept and others cannot. This problem will not die when I die, and we all need to be equipped in the future in case it happens again to a friend or loved one.

Enough preaching about acceptance. I'm sure many of you are wondering what this letter is all about. I was talking to my parents about it, and I thought it would be a good idea to keep everyone updated on my condition and changes in the system, etc. This is not only to keep the lines of communication open between us all, but also, these letters will act as a record of my progress, and you can show them to younger generations in order to give them insight to this illness.

I think everyone knows that I had a pretty scary summer this year. I had a sinus infection that lasted for about two months. During that time, I kept hurting my back from coughing so much, and I lost ten pounds. I am now over the cold, but I am still trying to gain back the weight.

Let me tell you a little about t-cells. T-cells are the leaders in your body against infection. They tell all the other cells where to go and what to fight. When you are born, your thymus serves as a t-cell factory, but once the job is done, they close the factory. So a normal body has a t-cell count of about 1200 to 1500 t-cells per whatever. The AIDS virus attacks t-cells, so the body doesn't know what to do. It's a very ingenious little bug. As it destroys cells, your body gets weaker and is more prone to disease. Depending on where the illness is in your body, what t-cells you have left are going to be there fighting, so your cell count drops when they draw blood during an infection. This summer was scary for me because my t-cell count

1

fell to 14! In August, they had doubled back up to 31, and
studies show that if you can keep them above 50, you can usually
avoid infection. I know the numbers sound really grim, but keep
in mind that I know one guy with a t-cell count of 2 and he's
been like that for two years. Mental attitude has a lot to do
with your health in this illness.

'I started taking an experimental drug called ddC. It is free
and coming from the government, and those of you who are familiar
with my political views will know that it makes me a little
uncomfortable being a guinea pig for the government. But, the
medicine is working. Although I don't know my t-cell count right
now, all my other blood counts are rising and I'm gaining weight.
I feel fine and have more energy than I have had in 6 months.

I'm sure you are all familiar with the Kim Bergalis story.
Although I know what happened to her is a tragedy, please keep in
mind that she has become very bitter in her final days. She does
not represent the views of most of us with AIDS, and her
endorsement of the Mandatory testing bill is only going to cause
people to lose their jobs, run up expenses, and instill a sense
of false security. A tip-off to the inablity of this bill to
address the real issues (health care workers are really the ones
at risk, not the patients) is the fact that the bill is being
sponsored by William Dannemyer from California. He has fought
tooth and nail to try to get quarantines in that state. He also
opposes any federal money going toward AIDS education. I urge all
of you to write a letter to your congressmen and get this bill
stopped. It will destroy the fragile health care system we have.
Things are already too precarious.

I have been speaking to church groups lately, which is where
I think the compassion and care needs to come from anyway. It
makes me very happy to know that I am having an affect on people,
helping them understand, helping them change their thinking. I
think I'll always be a crusader for this cause. Tomorrow, I am
going up to Camp Mitchell atop Petit Jean Mountain in order to
speak to 250 Episcopal teenagers. They are the ones in danger the
most right now, especially the teen girls. The boys don't want to
take the responsibility to protect their partners, and the girls
are left with all the blame if anything happens. And if you think
AIDS is bad, imagine having an infant born with the virus. If you
need to talk to your teens, please do so frankly. Believe me, in
today's modern society, there are no words they haven't heard.
You wouldn't believe some of the frank questions I get. If you
have trouble discussing it, contact your local Health department,
and they can point you toward an educational process that could
even include your school or church, or maybe just one on one.

Many of you wanted to know what you could do to help. I am
asking you to educate the people around you. Do not make this
disease into a "dirty little secret". Educate yourselves, get
involved, talk about your doubts and fears and hopes. The
greatest thing you can do, you have already done. By showing your
support for me, you have been brave in a world that does not
always recognize your type of bravery. This is a battle and we
must fight together. I am always willing to talk about this, and
I will talk to anyone who needs to hear more.

2

I hope this letter hasn't been too preachy, but I just wanted to establish a few facts about how the disease affects me and my life, as well as let you know that almost all of you came through when you were needed and lended support. If anything should ever happen to me, I want those of you who came out and gave support to know that you were loved and appreciated. You mean a lot to me. And most of all, you mean a lot to my family. This will be heavy on the hearts of Mama, Daddy, Steve, and Jim long after I'm gone. They need to know now that you are willing to be brave and be a part of the solution, not the problem.

School is keeping me on my toes, as well as my activist work, and I'll update all of you on my progress at the end of October Feel free to write me if you want because I love getting letters. God bless you all!

Love,

December 8, 1991

Dear Kith and Kin,
    It has been a long, stressful, yet rewarding month for me.
There have been a lot of wonderful things going on.
    The U.S. has changed forever because of what Magic Johnson
had to say. Regardless of whether or not you think he is heroic
for his admission, I think we can all agree that his visibility
will help in the fight against AIDS. I hope he not only tries to
educate everyone he can, but that he use his power to exert a
little influence in the White House.
    I know that since Magic made his announcement, people have
been talking to each of you about AIDS, you know, office talk and
school talk and church chat. I know it isn't easy to talk about
it objectively when you can't be objective because of me or
someone else you may know with AIDS. Now you see what PWA's are
up against all the time. We are not noticeable as PWA's by sight,
and often people talk to us about AIDS without knowing who we
are. It's a strange feeling, but I don't have a problem dealing
with it. I don't think wearing a sign would help. Anyway, I hope
that all this talk recently and public debate has helped each of
you in some way to deal with my illness. That's the best I can
hope for as an AIDS educator.
    The events of last weekend were hectic and stressful, but
ultimately rewarding. It was World AIDS Day on Sunday, and there
was a display in the Arkansas Arts Center of the Quilt, also
known as the Names Project. The Quilt is made up of panels
representing those who have died from AIDS. It started off with
only 1400 panels. It is now so big that they can no longer
display it as one piece, they have to mail different sections to
different events. Panels were added concerning people from
Arkansas in a moving ceremony. Also, we all pitched in and
created a mock cemetery in McArthur Park. It had quite an impact
on everyone who saw it.
    For those of you who don't regularly read Arkansas' only
statewide paper, I have been lambasted by the managing editor for
a political action of civil disobedience. It is safe to say two
things:
    He was wrong to think I was responsible.
    I seem to be in good company.
    Some people have come up to me and said that I should be
honored to be on the opposite side of John Robert Starr. I wish
he had not mentioned me personally, but I am glad we got him to
admit his prejudice. He stated that he wants nothing to do with
people with AIDS. I just think it's a little irresponsible for
the editor of the state's only paper to encourage such blatant
discrimination. Well, that 's the political side of me coming

1

out, and most of you know, or have come to know recently, that I'm a little to the left. Actually, a lot to the left. Maybe radical. But hey! It's radical times!

School is down to finals and I am very glad this semester is finally over. Being in the hospital really took a lot out of me, and I have difficulty catching back up. I think I'll remain in school next semester, but I won't be taking many classes. I have been trying to lead a "normal" life too hard, when I need to realize that my body just can't take the stress that it once could, or should be able to take. It's like being 26 in a 76 year old body. I have leg aches and I take naps. I get winded on stairs and I get a little from social security every once in a while. To be honest, I would rather be a 76 years old in a 26 year old body.

I have been having the usual health problems, all of which are more annoying than painful or dangerous. But my mental state is really good right now. I am a major Christmas fan, and this looks like it is going to be a great year. Nothing thrills me more than seeing all those people piling in rooms and filling all the chairs and sharing and laughing and talking about everything and anything. All the kids are bigger than last year, the television is one long bowl game, the house smells like the tree. I think this is a great time for all of us to celebrate our families. Whether it is you child, your spouse, your parent, or friends that are family as well, we all need to take the time and realize how lucky we are to have each other. I know too many who have no family left and are sick this year. I can't wait to get home this year so I can have a break from all of it. And I just hope everyone understands how wonderful and life-affirming our family is. We can get through anything.

I know some of you might be thinking in the back of your heads that there is the possibility that this is my last Christmas. I want you to know its okay to think about such things, but you should always remember that this could be any one of us. I mean, none of us have a guarantee that we'll be around tomorrow, much less a year from now. Sometimes I catch myself thinking about the "last" this or the "last" that, but I always snap out of it. If there is one thing we can learn from Christmas that cuts through all the commercialism it is that hope is born to us. We always have hope, and there is always hope to cling to. I knew a guy who lived with full-blown AIDS for 8 years, and I don't think he lived that long by counting his days and planning his funeral. He fought back and tried to stay happy, and he hoped for the best. I will always keep hoping, and this time of the year is the best for feeling hopeful. So don't think about whether or not we'll all be here next year, let's just all be thankful we are here today.

I think that most of you will receive this letter before Christmas, I hope you do. I will be seeing most of the Stephens

side of the family tree, and I hope to see as many Toons as I
can. I love you all very much and hope that this is a peaceful
and hopeful holiday season for all of you!

Merry Christmas,

Andy

February 11, 1992

Dear Kith and Kin,

It has been a very busy new year around here. I have started off the new year with a greater sense of purpose and hopes of accomplishing great things before summer rolls around. We'll see how things shape up.

The Arkansas AIDS Foundation is finally putting me on their board. There has been a lot of politics going on where it doesn't belong, and the board had been operating for months without a PWA sitting on it. After attending the last meeting, I quickly discovered that they were not in tune with the PWA community. I hope that I can help get things back on track.

My speaking engagements are getting more frequent and more fun. I am really enjoying my life as an activist and I am happy to be doing the work I do. To date, I've spoken to almost 2,000 people now, most teenagers. I spoke recently to the entire 8th grade of Hot Springs, the Rotary Club of Stuttgart, the ministerial staff at Baptist Hospital, and inpatients at the VA Hospital's Substance Abuse Program.

My proudest moment was speaking in Crossett last month. I got up early, very early, on a snowy Saturday morning to get down there on time. The other speaker who was following me down there wound up in a ditch and had to turn back to Little Rock. Undaunted in my four-wheel drive, I spoke to about 60 people from all over the community gathered at Holy Souls Chapel. I thought it would be emotional for me to speak in front of members of my hometown crowd, but I handled it pretty well. It isn't easy to get up in front of an audience and admit you have AIDS, much less to do so in front of your mother, your minister, and your second-grade teacher! I was well-received and I think that my message got through to people in a way that it has never done so before because they knew that I was one of them, I was from their town and I was affected by this epidemic. I am hoping that we will get into the schools there, where I have volunteered to speak to all the students. I am planning on presenting AIDS awareness to the staff of the school district on March 2nd, and we'll take it from there. It isn't easy to convince people of what they need to hear when they don't want to hear it.

The political front is warming up tremendously. Because of the national focus on Clinton, I have been besieged with phone calls from AIDS activists from all over the nation. The most recent came from New Hampshire. Everyone wants to know how we activists in Arkansas feel about Clinton's AIDS record. It is a touchy subject because there are so many in this state that don't want us to look bad on a national level, so they expect me to butter up the truth. Well, folks, I ain't gonna do it. The truth is that the state of Arkansas has never allocated a dime for AIDS funding. Clinton never introduced a comprehensive AIDS plan, and our schools have no set agenda for dealing with the problem. In truth, Hillary has been more vocal and visible in the fight against AIDS than her husband. Although he is touting a health care plan now, his past actions indicate that he is just flexing political muscle. The director of the State Health Department's AIDS Division was recently asked at a conference about how he felt about Clinton. He pointed out that Clinton had released • 30,000 dollars for testing and counseling from an emergency fund so the testing program wouldn't fold. The director said he thought that was encouraging. I stood up and spoke on behalf of those living with this disease and pointed out that after eleven years, 30,000 would hardly pay for one patient's medicine for six months, and that the fact it was released during his presidential campaign certainly makes it look like a political move. No sir, I said, we do not see that as encouraging. And we don't. Arkansas has the highest teen pregnancy rate in the country and we can't even teach teen girls how to protect themselves from that, much less disease and death.

Now the scary part of all of this is that I would vote for Clinton in a second if he got the nomination, not because he's so great, but it would be a vote against Bush. So that's where most of the AIDS activists in Arkansas stand on that issue.

As you will note from the return address, I have moved. I needed a smaller place with fewer bills, and I found a great place overlooking the Arkansas Arts Center and McArthur Park downtown. It should be cheaper, if I can just get through the move with my sanity. It is such a hassle. I should be moved in by the 15th of this month. My new phone number is yet unknown, but the folks in Crossett will have it soon and you can get it from them.

My health has been holding steady. My t-cell count dropped again, but that's no surprise. I have learned that it fluctuates all the time and that my body can handle low counts better than others. But still, I'd love to have a few extra t-cells laying around. Except for very dry skin, I have been fine. No new infections, no new problems. Let's hope that holds out for a while.

I'm hoping for a great spring and wishing the best for all of you. Keep me in your thoughts and prayers. I'll write again real soon.

Sincerely,

Dear Aunt Hazel,

I heard you weren't feeling well and I thought I would send you one of the cards my little company makes. This card is a prototype of the cards I will be producing this month.

This photograph was taken at an old cemetery in Vicksburg. I use a technique called sepia toning that turns the print antique brown. It really gives it an old-fashioned look. I and my business partner, David, do all of the production from printing to the photographs to mounting them and signing each one. In September, however, the business will be mine exclusively. It should help me get through school without starving.

I have one of your decorated bottles at my apartment. People are always telling me how much they like it. I have decorated an old phone in "Hazelesque" style!

Hope you feel better! I'll see you next time I come home from Big D!

Love,
Andy

(This letter was transcribed from a handwritten one that Andrew wrote to his Aunt Hazel. The original letter is featured on the next page.)

Dear Aunt Hazel,

I heard you weren't feeling well and I thought I would send you one of the cards my little company makes. This card is a prototype of the cards I will be producing this month.

This photograph was taken at an old cemetery in Vicksburg. I use a technique called sepia toning that turns the print antique brown. It really gives it an old-fashioned look. I and my business partner, David, do all of the production, from printing the photographs to mounting them, and signing each one. In September, however, the business will be mine exclusively. It should help me get through school without starving.

I have one of your decorated bottles at my apartment. People are always telling me how much they like it. I have decorated an old phone in "Applesque" style!

Hope you feel better! I'll see you next time I come home from Big D! Love,

Andy

147

June 19th, 1993

Dear Steve & Jim,

In accordance with one of the final requests of Andrew O'Hearn Toon your mother and I went to Bear Lake in the Rocky Mountain National Park on Monday June 28th, 1993. About 50 feet past Station #15 we found a large rock protruding out into the lake. Some of Andy's ashes were cast into the lake as he had requested. The visits to Ester Park meant a lot to Andy. Monday June 28th, 1993 was a picture perfect day at Bear Lake. This fulfilled all of Andy's requests except for "something at the pond" and someday we will get the Island and causeway fixed in honor of Andy. His ashes are at Bear Lake, Stephens clan pond, a small container beneath his headstone at the cemetery.

When I think of Andy now, I remember the good times and laughter. Time has already erased the bad times or turned them around.

Above all things Andy loved his family, we had many hours of discussion and debate. Agreed and disagreed but always we talked...kept the lines of communication open.

In closing let me preach. Andy loved his parents, Andy loved his brother. Andy communicates. Always keep the lines of communication open. There are no friends and family where communication ceases.

Love,
Dad

(This letter was written by Andrew's father, Donald L. Toon to Andrew's brothers. The letter was written after Andrew's death. A copy of the original, handwritten letter can be found on the next page.)

D. L. Toon, M.D., P.A.
310 ALABAMA STREET
CROSSETT, ARKANSAS 71635
TELEPHONE 364-5762

7/19/93

Dear Steve & Jim,

In accordance with one of the final requests of Andrew O'Hearn Toon your mother & me went to Bear lake in Rocky mountain Nat'l park on monday June 28th, 1993. About 50 feet past Station #15 we found a large rock protruding out into the lake. Some of andys ashes were cast into the lake as he had requested. The visits to Estes Park meant a lot to andy. monday June 28, 1993 was a picture perfect day at Bear lake.

This fulfilled all of andys request except for "Something at the pond" & some day we will get the Island & causeway fixed in Honor of andy. His ashes are at Bear lake, Stephens clan pond & a small container beneath his headstone at the cemetery.

When I think of andy now I only remember the good times & laughter. Time has already erased the bad times or turned them around.

Above all things andy loved his family. We had many hours of discussion & debate. agreed & disagreed but always we talked --- kept the lines of communication open.

In closing let me preach. Andy loved his parents, andy loved his brothers. andy communicated. always keep the lines of communication open. There are no friends & family when communication ceases.

love

Dad

PHOTOGRAPHY

Aside from writing, Andrew was also a very avid photographer. These are a few examples of his photography.

BIOGRAPHY

Andrew O'Hearn Toon was born February 5th, 1965 to Donald and Nancy Toon. From birth, it was quite clear that he was destined to be a performer. His mother states, "Andy presented as a breech birth, so the doctor asked if I minded that a group of nursing students observed. As a new nurse graduate, I could hardly refuse, so he had his first audience". This love of performing followed Andrew into his childhood. He loved performing in plays and would learn everyone's parts just in case a position needed to be filled in. He was also very active in his hometown church, Crossett First United Methodist Church, and designed a banner that hung in the church foyer for several years.

Andrew flourished in elementary school, constantly devising games to play with his friends as he loved to have a crowd. He worked with the Crossett Little Theater Group and performed in several plays, especially musicals. He joined many youth organizations, including: Cub Scouts, Boy Scouts (he attended a jamboree through this organization in Washington D.C.), and the Eagle Scouts with his two brothers, Steve and Jim.

In middle school, Andy won a contest to paint a wall in the school cafeteria that stayed for several years. He also joined the school band as a drummer which led to him becoming the drum major in high school.

When Andrew joined high school, he gained a reputation for joining as many clubs as he could. This time was considered to be his "preppy period". He also traveled to Europe with a group of students also from Arkansas. The summer before his senior year was spent as an exchange student in Honduras. Andrew spent a lot of time traveling, actually. His family loved to take trips and had many exciting experiences while camping at their deer camp and even visiting Bear Lake in Colorado. Despite all of this traveling, Andrew had time to

help develop a school newspaper, titled the "News Disturber". Andrew was a member of the Foreign Language Club, Men's Service Club, Kantorei, Madrigals, and theatre. Along with the newspaper, Andrew was the editor of Literally Speaking and the Student Council president.

News DisTurbeR

created adn designed by Krista Bennatt an Andy toon

/Volume 1   "ALL THE NEWS THAT'S FIT TO KILL...filled with news and typos"

Little Rock Dissappers in "Board Zhuffle"
by Ima Wimp

In the midst of a controversy over the size of its bullboards,the entire city of Little Rock disappeerd at approxiamatlie 2:31:34.03 PM yesterday,
The metropolis was last seen near the home of Miss Ima Boozer, a known philanthropist of the worst kind.A city of similar of description was seen riding in the caboose of a train from mena To El paso.
The police suspect fowl play, but the real untold story is that something funny is going on. The runaway,s mother, known simply as "Little Rock's Mother",thinks he could be in South Sucotash with the Ron Reagan,jr. Ballet Conpamy.
Us at the DIsturber believe that other cites could follow siut. In a move to keep our "fair" city from taking a vacation, Crawsett's mayor, Moore White, says a police block has been placed on all rooads leading out uv Crewssett, and the ever-keen Protecters-of-the-Poeple are keeping their potatoes peeled for any town sisilar to Crowsitt trying to escape.
Our stAff really doesnt care or give a patoobie if Ckrawssett leaves or not,but we want you to know that it is a possibility.

Beaver Cleaver Cleav Murders Two Cleaver Injures Cleaver
by Eddie Haskell

Theodore Cleaver,13, has been found guilty of murder in the first degree in the slaughter of his parents, June and Ward, by means of a cleaver. He is also guilty of assualting Wallac e Cleaver with a cleever.
Theodore, known to most as Beave is being kept in the California State Prison For Little Creeps. Authorities are not clear as to a motive. In trying to establish one(a motive,that is) the police are attempting to question Wallace Ceaver, who is in a hospital somewhere, and is suffering from bigol' cuts.
"The little creep just went bonkers on us, what a goof."commented Wallace."I think he's been hanging around Larry Mondello to much."
Larry Mondello,a close friend of Beever's, is in prison on charges of shoplifting from "Fat Free Seafoodand BeEr Emporium."
Theodoer is only being aloowed be visited on ly by his wife ou of wedlock,Violet Rutherford.

Society (or something)
by Wanda Partyallthetime

Susy Queue held a birthday party for her dog,Poopsie,to celebrate the poodle recei spaying.tea and alpo was served and no guest were present, except Susys mother,who became ill from eating too much Alpo./// The 57th Procrast inators Convention has been postponed until futher notice./// The Crossett Nursing Home Will host the "O 80"Marathon Saturday morning to be held Monday at 2:00 PM. Funer al services foll /// A party will be held at the home of Mr. John Wilkes tommorrow afternoon at Twelve Oaks Plantation.Dress will be Formal.The wedding plans of Mr. Ashley Wilke: and his cousin Miss Melanie Hamilton are expectedto be announced. By invitation on Rhett!!!Only a civil war could stop a party like this.///The end of the world as will occure at the "Church of the Sanctified Band Pants" tonight about 9:00PM. The pastor said a surprise is due to all who bring all of their worldly goods. Details will be given tomorrow.

(continued somewhere else)

A rough draft page of *The News Disturber*, a high school paper that Andrew helped develop.

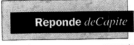

presents

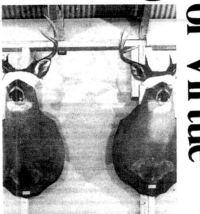

The Plague of Virtue

text by Andrew Toon
& William Shakespeare

December 7-10 & 14-17
Thurs-Sat shows start at 8 pm • Sunday shows at 2:30 pm

$7 • $5 students

Reponde deCapite has a new location
at 1217 South Broadway 1 block so. of the Broadway Car Wash
for ticket info: 376-6642

An advertisement for a play that Andrew wrote titled, "The Plague of Virtue".

Reponde's 'Plague' follows 'Lear,' sort of

By Lori Tucker
Gazette Staff

Shakespeare fans, beware — "King Lear" may never seem the same.

In "Plague of Virtue," Reponde de Capite takes the Shakespeare classic and, in the alternative theater's style, adapts it for modern times.

"It stays close to the 'King Lear' story line and it stays close to the point of Lear," Chuck Harvey, artistic director, said. But from Harvey's description of the performance, the differences may outweigh the similarities. Actual Shakespeare text is juxtaposed with scenes written by Drew Toon, an English major at the University of Arkansas at Little Rock, who is assistant director.

"It's very spectacle-orientated," Harvey said. And while spectacle is typical of Shakespeare, with Reponde that translates into multimedia effects, a stage which becomes a maze for the characters, a golfing scene and a session with a psychiatrist. All this gives it a "movie-like quality" and allows the company to play with the absurdity of situation, Harvey said.

The set, designed by David Bailin, adds to the tension as it visually depicts Lear's world turning upside down, Harvey said.

One of the biggest twists may well be the reduction of the cast to only three actors, each depicting three characters. With a mixture of acting styles, different voices and costuming, Harvey said he believes

Fast Facts

■ The Plague of Virtue," by Reponde de Capite, 1217 S. Broadway, will be presented at 8 p.m. Thursday, Friday, Saturday, and Dec. 14, 15 and 16, and at 2:30 p.m. Dec. 10 and Dec. 17. Tickets are $7 for adults and $5 for students. Call 376-6642 for reservations.

it will be established in moments who is who when.

Norman Green plays Lear, Gloucester and Fool; Gigi Kagy plays Goneril, Regan and Edmund; and Andrew Cuk plays Kent, Cordelia and Edgar.

Toon's title "The Plague of Virtue" comes from his interpretation of the theme of "King Lear." "I feel that the downfall of all the 'pure' characters came about through their inability to deceive or lie," Toon said in a press release.

"Like a disease, goodness consumed and destroyed them. In fact, the entire plot is set in motion by Cordelia's inability to lie. Sometimes virtue can be your worst enemy, regardless of what you are taught in childhood. For Cordelia, virtue brought only injustice and death, traits which most people find unattractive to say the least," he continued.

Reponde has moved to a new location, 1217 S. Broadway, one block south of the Broadway Car Wash. Harvey said parking is available on nearby side streets.

A review of "The Plague of Virtue" that was published in the Arkansas Gazette.

In 1989, Andrew was published in the *Arkansas Times*, winning Honorable Mention in the magazine's photo contest. He had submitted a photograph of a headboard and footboard that were in his aunt's barn.

Michael Cobb recently graduated from Arkansas State University with a degree in accounting; he works for a private club in Jonesboro. His honorable-mention photo is of his daughter, Casey, wearing a hat they bought in Overton Square in Memphis at "Crazy Hat Night." Cobb used a flash with existing light to create the effect.

Andrew Toon of Crossett will be a student at the University of Arkansas at Little Rock this fall; he's interested in both writing and photography. This photo shows a headboard and footboard, bought in 1936, that are now in his aunt's barn in Crossett. Toon says, "I wander around her barn because it's really good therapy photographically."

ARKANSAS TIMES · 37

During Andrew's college years, he attended three different schools including: Hendrix University, the University of Arkansas at Fayetteville, and the University of Arkansas at Monticello. Like many college students, he changed his major several times before graduating. He loved to plan parties and also loved to participate in family reunions and holidays.

Andrew grew up having to help on a farm that was owned by his parents, along with his brothers. Understandably, he and his brothers did not like to be called "farm hands". So, they came up with the title of Farm Maintenance Technicians as an official job description. His mother believed that that was Andy's idea since he always did have a way with words. Asides from that Andrew had a variety of jobs including: a clothing store clerk, a helper in a frame shop, a hairdresser, and a bookstore clerk. He especially enjoyed his job as a

bookstore clerk due to the fact that Bill Clinton would frequent the bookstore with his daughter, Chelsea.

Andrew was also a political activist and took on the political world as his own personal challenge. He wrote many letters to government officials regarding various political issues. Once he even got into a heated discussion with his surgeon who was performing a surgical procedure on him at the time – under local anesthesia, of course.

In the early 1990s, Andrew developed a greeting card business with a group of friends called "Urbanese". The business itself never really took off and was more of a learning experience.

urbanese

"a language of ideas native to the urbane"

The logo for Andrew's greeting card business.

The last years of his life, after he contracted AIDS, were spent working with such groups as RAIN (Regional AIDS Interfaith Network) and the AIDS Brigade which he helped organize. His mother remembers a moment during the last week of his life, "he was getting very weak, I was attending him and adjusted his IV when he opened his eyes and said – Mama, you really need to do something with your hair. He could always make me laugh".

Even after he contracted the disease that later killed him, Andrew never lost his faith in God and remained optimistic until the end. He died on December 22nd, 1992. His ashes were buried at Crossett Lakewood Cemetery on July 30th, 1993 and a Toon Family monument was put in place. His family believes that he was a blessing in so many ways and are thankful for his full life.

This is an AIDS quilt that was made in honor of Andy. It features his silly ties and sun tattoo that he had on his arm. It has been featured throughout the U.S.

REMARKS FROM FAMILY & FRIENDS

FROM BETTY, WES, AND CARLA:

Nancy,

When I explained to Carla what you were doing for Andy, she wanted to talk it through. In my opinion, she was very interested in learning the meaning of a "tribute remembrance." With that in mind, the first thing she said was

Carla: ..."he was so funny....he and Kathryn were always laughing and making funny faces" (feel free to use her name, I think she would like that).

Wes: "I always thought of Andy as a free spirit."

Betty: "Andy had a laugh, a smile, and a greeting for everyone.....one of my cherished memories is how he championed so many causes like working to obtain salt and pepper on the tables in the high school cafeteria....and, of course, he succeeded! When Wes and I attended the memorial service for Andy in Little Rock, it was amazing to see the cross section of people whom Andy touched with his interests, comedic humor, and ability to spread joy with his artistic eye for beauty and gift of words."

FROM JERRIE HOPPER DOMINIQUE:

I was half grown before I realized Andy wasn't actually my cousin! He kept my secrets, he didn't laugh when I was humiliated. He was a willing participant in childhood adventures. He could empathize with me in my plight of younger, quieter sibling to an outgoing, cool older sibling. He was good and he was kind and I loved him. All our lives are diminished because he is no longer with us.

From PATTI:

Igor Stravinsky said, "In order to create there must be a dynamic force, and what force is more potent than love?" From these works, you will no doubt see Andy's creativity. What those who knew him also saw was his great love. Love for his family, his friends and strangers never met. The last time I sat with him, I was an adult but quite naive. We sat on a mountain until three in the morning - talking. I thought we were talking, but in fact, he was teaching me, with love, about life. He knew he was lucky to be the exception and be loved beyond measure, but he taught me about other sons who did not have that kind of love and walked alone through the most difficult times in their lives. He wanted me to know how to deal with the risks my own children might face as they grew to adulthood. As Andy said, "It's not a matter of right or wrong. It's a matter of life and death." Thank you, Andrew, Andy, Drew, Cousin, and although our time together was too short, I am so blessed for that last night and to have known you.

From LEE MULLET:

When Ellen and I visited Crossett, Andy was our leader in every activity. He was a fountain of ideas for fun. Shooting bottle rockets at cows, taking apart a dead snake, digging a four foot deep mud hole in the pasture, making forts in rooms, playing Monopoly, dressing up and putting on a show, watching Monty Python--he was always planning the next thing we would do.

From SUSANNE:

My memories of Andy are really few and far between because of our age difference. I was away in college, then married and moved away for almost all of his growing up years. I do have vivid memories of all that red hair on the Toon boys. And I also remember Steve and Andy being in my wedding in July 1971!

Andy with his cousins, Jim, Ellen, and Lee

From BUDDY STEPHENS:

One of my best memories of Andy was when he was drum major for the "CHS Marching 100" (I think the number was closer to 125) during the mid-1980s. Along with Andy's leadership and the help of band director, C.T. Foster, I feel the band was one of the best (if not the best in Arkansas at the time). People would come to the football games just to watch the band perform, not the ball game.

From AUNT ALICE AND UNCLE TOM

Our daughters, Lee and Ellen grew up with Andy, and we all loved him – not just because he was family but also because he made us laugh. The room lightened up when he walked in the door. We spent a lot of weekends in Crossett while I was single. The minute I parked the car at my Mamma's house, the girls would jump out and head to Nancy's house 100 years away. The next time I would see them they would have Andy in tow and more likely than not would have mud up to their knees and hay in their hair.

They would put on plays, build tent rooms between the beds and

generally make messes.

When I got transferred and Alice and I moved to Denver, Andy came to visit and to go skiing with us. The pictures below illustrate that, to them, it was not just how you skied but how you looked that was cool. We had a great time.

Andy was a great photographer. He had an eye for visualizing a picture and then the knowledge to use the camera to capture the image with perfect light and focus. After Andy got sick he faced his condition with unbelievable insight and bravery. Sometimes a man shows the most strength when the body is weakest.

We loved you Andy, think of you often, and miss you greatly.

From JOHN HOLLIMON:

(This is a sermon titled, "The Definition of a Stranger", that was given by Mr. Hollimon)

Bill Clinton was a president who brought forth strong feelings in everyone. Perhaps his greatest legacy will be the idea that, "it all depends on the definition".

When we think of strangers how, exactly, are to define that concept?

According to Mr. Webster a stranger is one who is foreign or alien. One in the house of another as a guest. One who is un-known. In a word...other. As an aside, it is interesting that we refer to the one with whom we are closest as our significant other. If they are significant to us, how can they be other?

Rather than talk about strangers from without today, I want to spend a few minutes with the idea of the strangers within.

A few weeks ago, Charlotte and I, along with our daughters, a son-in-law, and our first grandchild went for the Centennial Celebration of the First United Methodist Church in Crossett. We were members of that congregation for fourteen years. In that fourteen years, there was a stranger in our midst.

We thought we knew Andy, all of us, one of us. He was a boy, smart and funny, involved in all aspects of the life of the church. He was a teenager, in the Sunday School class I taught, one who actually knew the answers, at least some of them. He went on a mission trip to Central America and we heard his stories when he returned. Andy went to college and didn't return. But word came back. Andy became Drew and he came out of the closet.

Suddenly, Andy became a stranger. We didn't know Drew. He was other. His family was there, we silently acknowledged their situation, we gathered close around them. Drew was rarely mentioned.

It was when Drew became ill that he taught me one of the most important lessons of my life. At the time we knew enough about AIDS to fear it, but not much more than that. It took Drew slowly. His parents, a doctor, and a nurse were as powerless as the rest of us to change its course. Drew died, bravely, as he lived. But it was not his dying that was the lesson for me. Watching his parents, as they cared for him, as they came to terms with his life, I realized that Drew was still Andy, still one of us. And that strangers are only strange for as much as we make them separate from us.

It all depends on how you define the word.

From STEPHEN P. TOON Ph.D.:

Andrew O'Hearn Toon - My Brother

How to start? I could start with pain but that would be selfish. I could start with tragedy but that would be a disservice. I could start with celebration but that would be trite. I think I will start with Love because even now 25 years later that has grown. There are things now that I understand which I could not understand years ago. Strength, character, compassion, honor and a sense of right and wrong that transcends the boundaries of shallow thinking commonly associated with today's politics. I Love my brother and what knowing him continues to mean to me today.

My brother Andy understood more about the South, family, hunting, fishing and people in general that anyone I have known. It was almost like him having an extra sensory perception. The beauty of this knowledge was that he could express it in humor and with insight that could make it available to others (albeit often with a sarcastic vent). I remember the political discussions we had around the dinner table which he used to always win. Each photograph he took showed the insight into the simple things that few could see until he captured it.

He had a sense of right and wrong that allowed him to truly see things that frankly I feel Jesus tried to teach us. He dreamed of bigger things while respecting the common things that bind us together. He looked to a life of no boundaries at a time when we seem to have been bounded by our own shortcomings. He dreamed of a world where people could be there best. He liked pop culture but respected the past. He saw dark things in hypocrisy but could find beauty in the life surrounding him.

I recall one morning before the opening of deer season. He did not care to hunt but fully understood and engaged in the ritual. I was singing in the early morning and he joined in excited about the chase, the sounds, and the smells that are as ancient as man himself. Oddly enough it was that moment I think I truly understood him and there was a bond created that only brothers can have.

He was the drum major, the writer, political activist, trendsetter, son, friend, insider and outsider. He was reasonable and irrational. He was an Arkansas Farm Boy and a Dallas City Boy.

He is my brother.

Andy with his two brothers, Stephen and Jim

From NORMA:

Our family always called him Andy, though some of his friends called him Drew. By any name, I remember him as a sweet, funny and passionate young man who left us much too soon.

Andy was creative and would collaborate with others to write a skit or other entertainment for our family gatherings. We looked forward to the productions! He was keenly observant and could make us laugh at our individual foibles and idiosyncrasies. One of his writings which he did following the death of a family member was particularly moving for me. His attention to mundane details during the family rituals evoke memories of the event as well as the awareness that life goes on – as it must – even as we mourn our loss. I miss him.

From A COUSIN:

I was in the next older generation of the Toon boys, but remember hearing of pranks that they loved to pull on others.

There was a twinkle in Andy's eye that reflected humor, intelligence and such artistic ability.

From NANCY HOPPER DANNHEIM:

There are so many memories of the Toon boys, that they sometimes run together. Our families spent so much time together. We hunted together, we fished Lake Chicot on a barge, we camped, we laughed, and most of all we loved. Steve and I were the closest, because of age, but Andy and my little sister were always there, somewhere! We talked them into so many things and had them cover for us, if the need arose!! We truly had a good working relationship! Andy was special. He was sweet and kind and I loved him very much. I probably didn't show that often enough and I truly regret it. Andy will always be in my heart and hold a super special place there. I wish we could go back....for just one day!

"If thou shouldst never see my face again, pray for my soul."
-Alfred, Lord Tennyson

ABOUT THE AUTHOR

Andrew O'Hearn Toon was a writer, photographer, and activist. When he wasn't spending time with his family or the numerous amount of organizations that he was a part of, he was creating and thinking. When he died in 1992 he left behind a substantial amount of work that never saw publication. The bulk of this work included poetry that showcased the famous wit he possessed and interesting way of thinking about the world. Andrew was the type of man who never shied away from fighting for a cause he believed in. This characteristic proved especially true after he contracted AIDS. No matter how debilitating the disease was he maintained his efforts with RAIN in finding a cure for the disease. This book serves as vessel for preserving his memory and talent.

Made in the USA
Middletown, DE
01 February 2019